The Mesopotamian Tale

An Origin Story

Revised Edition

Mike Brenner

Revised Edition

Copyright © 2021
By Mike Brenner

All rights reserved. This book may not be reproduced in whole or in part, or transmitted in any form, without written permission from the publisher except by a reviewer who may quote brief passages in a review; nor may any part of this book be reproduced, stored in a retrieval system or transmitted in any form or by any means electronic, mechanical, photocopying, recording or any other without written permission from the publisher.

ISBN: 978-0-578-63077-9

Intentions Books
239 Main Street
Reisterstown, MD
21136

Illustrations by Author
Cover by Sandy Carlsen-Rougeux
Production Services by Clark Thomas Riley
Printing and Distribution by IngramSpark

Table of Contents

Dedication

Introduction 1

The Mesopotamian Tale 3

The Mesopotamian Tale With Commentary 18

Epilogue 43

Dedication

To the memory of my parents

Fred and Nancy Brenner

Introduction

THE MESOPOTAMIAN TALE, compact companion to *Evolution Diverted*, contains the story that's at the heart of that weighty book. The story, woven from texts and images unearthed from the ruins of ancient Mesopotamian cities (in present day Iraq), covers the age that began with remarkable events leading to the birth of our kind … and that ended as the religion of the olden gods, civilization's first faith, faded out.

The *Tale* confronts the conventional view of the literature of Mesopotamia peoples by taking the accounts of the gods at face value, that is, by accepting that the Mesopotamian deities were huge, powerful, flesh and blood humanoids who'd come to Earth, not fictional characters in sagas about totally imaginary gods.

The accounts brought together to form this narrative, when they were first discovered, were spread over many thousands of artifacts. Piecing together texts originally separated by time and distance and then assembled and translated by numerous scholars, was a process based in an intuitive feel for a vital narrative. That narrative has until now been obscured by the piecemeal nature of the source texts; by the dramatic, poetic style of those texts; and by the destructive effects of war and weather. The work involved as much art as scholarship. This author hopes, nevertheless, that in time experts will confirm that *The Mesopotamian Tale* has been accurately and truthfully abstracted from the vast archaeological findings.

In the book *Evolution Diverted*, the *Tale* is explored at length, citing source material and relevant science. In contrast, this book's commentary is brief, aiming to show just one thing: how the *Tale* lays bare the roots of the suffering through the ages caused by war, exploitation, and tyranny. This book doesn't try to bolster the credibility of the narrative it presents nor try to show how our troubled state would be relieved if we were to emerge from mass amnesia. Those tasks are taken up in *Evolution Diverted*.

The ancient land we call Sumer, in what now southern Iraq, was known in its time as SHU.MER, meaning *Land of the Watchers*. Acknowledging the initial Middle Eastern consonant of its archaic name, we'll refer to the land as Shumer.

This work's commentary focuses on two pivotal moments: the time when monotheism was rising to replace the worship of the gods; and the present time, when we are making choices that will determine the fate of our species and our world.

A cylinder seal image illustrating the narrative in *Chapter V: Crisis on Earth*. It shows Ninmach, mother goddess, holding the first human infant, laboratory assistants with equipment, and a tree of life.

The Mesopotamian Tale

Chapter I: ANOTHER PLANET In the cold of deep space, far, far from the Sun, dwells a now forgotten member of our family of planets. Once every 3,600 years, like a comet, it comes near. This planet was famous in Mesopotamia for the fateful way it crossed the inner Solar System. In fact, one of its many names was The Planet of the Crossing, NI.BI.RU, in Shumerian, the first language of Mesopotamia. The Planet was riveting when it approached, for NI.BI.RU appeared as a great golden orb, its brilliance rivaling the Sun.

To the Mesopotamians the planets were powerful bodies of consciousness, celestial deities. With its majestic orbit and its brilliance, NI.BI.RU was deemed to rule the Solar System. As it passed by, if The Planet of the Crossing didn't come close, there could be drama in the heavens, but nothing more. Yet if NI.BI.RU came too near, it would disrupt Earth's atmosphere, crust, and ocean. This was a god to be reckoned with.

Chapter II: COLLISION The Mesopotamians knew that in the distant past, a water-rich, life-supporting planet had existed, circling the Sun between Mars and Jupiter. Their name for that world was TI.AM.AT, meaning Maiden Who Gives Life. When NI.BI.RU made its transits of the Solar System, it crossed the ecliptic, the plane in which all the other planets spin, in the same way every time: it always transected the path of TI.AM.AT. On one fateful crossing, NI.BI.RU came so close to TI.AM.AT that one of its moons crashed into her, tearing off a portion of her crust. The impact drove TI.AM.AT into an orbit closer to the Sun. Wounded and relocated, TI.AM.AT earned another epithet: KI, meaning Hollowed Out. In the orbit that had been TI.AM.AT's, the rocky debris from the collision spread out, forming a ring.

The creation epics of Mesopotamia speak of the collision as a battle between two powerful deities, NI.BI.RU, a hero avenger, and TI.AM.AT, a miscreant troublemaker. In the words of the epic from Babylonia:

[heroic Nibiru] tore Tiamat's [bottom part] to form the great band as a hammered bracelet

Chapter III: CRISIS ON NIBIRU The Planet of the Crossing is home to an advanced humanoid race, tall beings living immensely long lives. The surface of their sunless world was made habitable by a reflective golden shell high in its atmosphere.

An environmental crisis loomed: the golden shell was failing, but the planet's gold supplies were depleted. An explorer had earlier found gold on Earth. An expedition was organized. If enough of the mineral could be mined on Earth and sent back home, the crisis could be averted. The king of NI.BI.RU, AN, meaning Heavenly One, chose as leader of the mining colony the eldest of his sons, a prince born to his concubine. A gifted scientist and engineer, he would be called EN.KI, meaning Lord of the Earth. This took place about four hundred fifty thousand years ago ... long before the age of man.

EN.KI, firstborn of divine An, led the colonists as their "great brother"; taught them metallurgy, brick making, building construction, and shipbuilding; made the Tigris and Euphrates navigable and clear; connected the rivers with a canal; and opened waterways in the marshes. (A major Shumerian poem in EN.KI's voice lauds these accomplishments.)

Chapter IV: SETTLING ON EARTH In Shumerian, the settlers were called the AN.UN.NA.KI, Those of Heaven Who Are on Earth. In Akkadian, the next language to develop in the region and the first of the Semitic tongues, they were the I.LU, the Lofty Ones. The colonists called their first settlement E.RI.DU, meaning Home Faraway. The region surrounding E.RI.DU was E.DIN, meaning Home of the Righteous Ones.

EN.KI determined that gold mining would be successful. AN sent more colonists, led by a son with his queen, a prince outranking EN.KI in prestige. He would be called EN.LIL, meaning Lord of the Command. Tensions developed. EN.KI, founder of the colony and AN's firstborn, was unwilling to yield leadership to EN.LIL as his father asked. AN, prepared to lead the colony himself and to make one of the brothers viceroy on NI.BI.RU, travelled to Earth to see the fraternal dispute resolved. The three royals drew lots and EN.LIL was the winner. Authority over the colony was to be divided. EN.KI would be chief of all technical matters, lord of the oceans, and EN.LIL's subordinate.

Just below EN.LIL and EN.KI in a social system of many ranks were ten AN.UN.NA.KI nobles. Together they constituted a ruling council of twelve, six male, six female. The AN.UN.NA.KI were astrologers, and to them the number twelve governed the Solar System. A circle of twelve governing Lofty Ones would benefit their society by aligning it with the celestial order.

Though EN.KI did at times defy EN.LIL's orders, most disagreements between the brothers were well managed. Dynastic opposition, though, was a fact of life on NI.BI.RU, and it soon characterized the culture of the Earth colony. The descendants of EN.KI claimed that their clan's rights had been usurped when EN.LIL was made supreme ruler. Conflicts over power and prestige arose frequently between descendants of the brothers. Aristocrats came into fierce, jealous opposition, leading to endless battles waged for rights, glory, and riches.

Chapter V: CRISIS ON EARTH

Golden ingots were flown to NI.BI.RU every 3,600 years, when the shining planet approached. The mines and smelters in southern and eastern Africa were in full production. The working conditions in the mines, however, were brutal. Suddenly, having borne a hard fate for a very long time, the ordinarily obedient commoners had had enough, and mutinied. A Babylonian epic begins with these words:

when the gods like men bore the work and suffered the toil the gods' toil was great the work was heavy the distress was much ... suffered the toil day and night ... complaining backbiting grumbling

NI.BI.RU was still in need of gold. EN.LIL left E.DIN to see for himself what was happening in the mines and was taken hostage. The epic continues, quoting the leader of the rebellion:

Let us adopt hostilities and battle ... the lofty ones heeded his words they set fire to their tools ... at the gate of the hero enlil ... some shouted let us kill him ... break the yoke

AN came to Earth and convened a council. EN.LIL said he'd resign and return to NI.BI.RU unless the leader of the mutiny was executed, but to AN, the miners' case was compelling. He insisted that a solution be found.

EN.KI envisioned a way to resolve the impasse. He'd observed hominin creatures in the nearby wilds, small and primitive, yet similar to their own race in many ways. He boldly proposed a solution: he would use AN.UN.NA.KI "essence" to modify the native creatures for service in the mines. His partner in the laboratory effort would be NIN.MACH, meaning Great Lady, half-sister to himself and to EN.LIL, a scientist and royal midwife. Gaining EN.LIL's grumpy consent, AN told the pair to proceed. In the words of the creation epics...

let [Ninmach] fashion a worker
let a workman bear the toil of the lofty ones
let her create a mixed worker let him bear the yoke ...
[all that is needed is to] bind upon [the creature] the image of the gods it can be done ...

*they summoned and asked the goddess the midwife
of the gods ... you are the birth goddess ... make a
primitive worker ... let him bear the yoke assigned
by Enlil*

*let primitives be crafted after [a god's] pattern
out of his blood they fashioned mankind
it was a work beyond comprehension ...*

*in the essence god and man shall be bound to a unity
brought together so that in the end of days the flesh
and the soul which in a god have ripened that soul
in a blood kinship be bound*

After a prolonged time of trial and error, the new race was born. EN.KI's wife was the first surrogate birth mother. Next, fourteen female AN.UN.NA.KI served as surrogates. So ...

*[Ninmach] nipped off fourteen portions of essence ...
into the wombs of the twice-seven birth goddesses
the mother goddess put the mixed essence ...
the fateful tenth month was approaching ...
she opened the womb her face brightened with joy ...
that which was in the womb came forth*

NIN.MACH was revered in Mesopotamia for her role in the birth of humankind. She was also known as MAM.MU, meaning Mother Goddess, and as NIN.TI, meaning Lady Life.

Finally, EN.KI was able to give the servant race fertility, but not the long lifespan of the Lofty Ones.

With his own seed [Enki] made the perfect ... earthling ... with [knowing] he perfected him to him he had given knowing lasting life he did not give

Chapter VI: GIANTS IN THE EARTH The new Earthmen were distinct from the two species that had been blended to bring them into existence, the four-to-five-foot-tall, dark, furry, forward-leaning African hominin, and the fair, seven-foot-tall, smooth-skinned, erect being from NI.BI.RU. Intermediate in height between the two, the human beings had features of each ... a head of dark terrestrial hair and a smooth alien skin, for example.

The AN.UN.NA.KI commoners in Mesopotamia asked that humans be brought out of Africa so that they, too, would be relieved of labor. EN.KI objected, so EN.LIL assaulted his compound. His attack succeeded. EN.LIL then took "black headed ones" to E.DIN, where they became laborers, farmers, builders, and cooks.

Cities were founded on the plain and uplands of the rivers Tigris and Euphrates, as settlement moved inland from ER.I.DU, which was near the head of the Persian Gulf, cities such as Ur, Lagash, Nippur, Kish, and Babylon. Enthralled with the tall, brilliant, skilled, beautifully clothed, fair Lofty Ones, the humans living in the cities, materially dependent, inferior physically as well as intellectually, short-lived, dark, and naked, did not need to be coerced into serving their superiors.

The AN.UN.NA.KI, flying from place to place and into the heavens in "sky chambers" and bearing "thunderbolt" weapons, claimed divinity for themselves. In fact, several of the most highly ranked of the Lofty Ones claimed to be the personifications on Earth of the celestial deities, the planets of the Solar System and the signs of the Zodiac.

The overall authority for each city rested with one of the twelve highest AN.UN.NA.KI lords. He and EN.LIL together appointed a noble of lesser rank to administer the city as its king. Kingship had been granted to the colony by AN. On NI.BI.RU AN's insignia were the tiara, for his royal stature; the scepter, for his power; and the shepherd's staff, for the guidance he provided. Replicas of the symbols of his authority were given to the kings on Earth.

Besides forming the laboring masses of the cities, humans were the foot soldiers in the armies of the Lofty Ones. For this role, too, no coercion was needed. To fight and die for one's beloved god and to kill the followers of his enemy were glorious deeds.

While the noble AN.UN.NA.KI males had female partners, hardly any of the commoners did. The ordinary AN.UN.NA.KI began to take human women as wives … resulting in an unplanned second round of hybridization between the terrestrial and celestial species. Many of the fruits of those unions had greater size, intelligence, and longevity than humans had ever known.

Chapter VII: DELUGE The AN.UN.NA.KI were thriving, supported in luxury by their enthralled human servants. But disaster loomed. The Lofty Ones learned that on its next passage NI.BI.RU would come close to Earth, wreak havoc and cause a watery catastrophe. Before the deluge would strike, the Lofty Ones could take to their spacecraft ... yet what of the humans?

EN.LIL had long before come to regard humankind as an abomination, out of disgust for the interbreeding between humans and AN.UN.NA.KI. He'd even tried to decimate civilized humanity, but EN.KI had blocked his cruel campaigns. Now a natural event was going to do the job for him ... as long as the people were kept in the dark. EN.LIL directed the ruling circle to swear an oath not to disclose the disaster to come, thus sealing the fate of the peoples of Mesopotamia. EN.KI at first refused the oath, but eventually gave in.

However, EN.KI couldn't actually accept the total annihilation of his Mesopotamian children. He designed a vessel that could save a few souls from the city of Shuruppak so that the population of civilized humanity could in time be restored. The craft would also carry "seeds of life", genetic material from Mesopotamia's animals and plants. He gave instruction to an esteemed devotee, using a trick to avoid overtly breaking the oath. Keeping the craft's true purpose secret, the follower enlisted help to build it.

This is the sequence of events in the flood epics of Mesopotamia • The golden planet approaches • The Anunnaki learn of the impending flood • A powerful gale blows from the south • A loud roar fills the air • Clouds darken the sky • The Lofty Ones ascend • After massive rains, comes a wall of water.

After NI.BI.RU passed over, the AN.UN.NA.KI watched in horror and grief as all they'd built and nurtured in Mesopotamia was obliterated.

the gods cowered like dogs crouched against the outer wall [of the craft a goddess] cried out like a woman in labor ... the anunnaki gods weep with her ...their lips drawn tight ... one and all

Ninti saw and she wept ... my creatures have become like flies they fill the rivers like dragonflies

As the water drained off, they spotted the vessel of salvation. EN.LIL was furious over the violation of the oath. He was urged by EN.KI and the others to relent, and he did, and pledged to never again harm humankind.

Chapter VIII: REBUILDING If the AN.UN.NA.KI were to once again have the way of life they'd been enjoying, the tasks ahead were staggering. As EN.KI and EN.LIL contemplated rebuilding the cities, restoring agriculture, and resuming gold shipments, they came to a momentous decision. No longer would humans be restricted to relatively low-level tasks. As the population was rebuilt, promising humans would be endowed with the knowledge and skills needed to restore and maintain civilization. There would be human scribes, scientists, technicians, teachers, artists, musicians ... and even kings, for AN decreed that kingship would again be granted to Earth. Each city would have its ruling Lofty One and he, as before, along with EN.LIL, would summon a king to the throne. Only now the sovereign would be a "man of renown", descended from the marriages of high-ranking AN.UN.NA.KI with humans also distinguished by lineage.

It would take time for the mud left by the flood to dry so that the cities could be rebuilt, food production could rise, and the population could be restored ... about four thousand years. A new spaceport, though, was needed quickly, because the two in Mesopotamia were buried deep in soft mud. In the central Sinai a base serving the AN.UN.NA.KI ruling Egypt had survived, but it was too distant from the settlements being restored. A new facility was built in the mountains to the west of Mesopotamia.

New cities were built on the sites of the buried settlements, their principal edifices built to conform to the plans and locations of the destroyed originals. Within a few hundred years of their construction, the cities had all the attributes of civilized life: wheeled vehicles and draft animals; boats of various types; canals for irrigation and transport; baked bricks and paved streets; libraries, temples, granaries, schools, and multi-story houses; various metals; fine textiles; domesticated stock, grains, and fruits; musical scales and instruments; judges and juries; civic administrations with bicameral legislatures; money, measures, and weights; commerce, customs duties, and financing; even board games.

The range of what the cities' scribes wrote is equally impressive: chronologies of dynasties and wars; essays about philosophy, geography, biology, and education; texts of advanced mathematics, astronomy, medicine, surgery, and pharmacology; epics, proverbs, poems, songs, and memoirs; guides for grammar and vocabulary; food and beverage recipes; marriage and *inheritance customs; court records and codes of criminal, family, and tax law; commercial records and contracts.*

Following the flood, the lands ruled by the AN.UN.NA.KI were divided among the great clans. Mesopotamia proper and its surrounds went to the sons of EN.LIL. Africa was to be ruled by the sons of EN.KI. The Indus Valley, in present day India, went to IN.AN.NA, granddaughter of EN.LIL. The zone around the Sinai spaceport wasn't assigned to either clan; it went to NIN.MACH. As sister to both royal brothers, it was hoped that she would be able to keep it neutral.

***Chapter IX: CONFLICT AND CATASTROPHE** The flood interrupted the noble AN.UN.NA.KI's violence. As the human population recovered, though, the ruling Lofty Ones rebuilt their armies and resumed their bloody ways.*

MAR.DUK, eldest son of EN.KI, made a startling announcement. His astrologic sign was Aries, the Ram, and since Earth was entering the Age of Aries, he proclaimed that it was time for him to ascend and be acknowledged as the chief of all the Lofty Ones.

Meaning to undo what he saw as the original theft of his father's rights by his uncle, MAR.DUK began drives of conquest, rousing fresh hostility between the two clans. EN.LIL was shocked when he realized that MAR.DUK intended to attack the Sinai spaceport ... and that his army appeared unstoppable.

The prospect of his belligerent nephew having control of one of the two launch facilities so alarmed EN.LIL that he resolved to deny MAR.DUK the base with the only means available: destroying it. Dismissing dire warnings from EN.KI, he empowered two of MAR.DUK's rivals to use the colony's hidden weapons of terror, seven powerful bombs. He also authorized the simultaneous destruction of five small cities just north of the Sinai, in hopes of killing MAR.DUK's son. In the battle epic, the attackers are called Annihilator and Scorcher.

annihilator to the [launch zone] set his course
the awesome seven without parallel trailed behind ...
he raised his hand the [zone] was smashed
the plain by the [zone] he obliterated...
then emulating annihilator ... scorcher the [road
on the gulf of aqaba] followed the cities he
finished to desolation he overturned them

In his fear and rage EN.LIL didn't envision the "cloud of death" the assault would spawn. Killing vapors drifted east with the prevailing winds, devastating - but not destroying - the cities of southern and central Mesopotamia. The near total collapse of Shumerian culture followed, documented in many lamentation texts:

[a god & his wife] hid in their ziggurat ...when they
finally left Ur they saw what had befallen the land
the people like potsherds filled the city streets ...
in its boulevards ... scattered they lay ...
on the banks of the Tigris and Euphrates...
sickly plants grow...all living creatures come to an end ...
the [cloud] has crushed the land, wiped out everything

on the land fell a calamity one unknown to man

one that had never been seen before
one that could not be withstood ...
it stands beside a man yet none can see it ...
there was no defending against the ... evil
which has assailed the land like a ghost ...
through the door like a snake it glides
through the hinge like a wind it blows in ...
those who fled to the streets were struck down in the streets ... cough and phlegm weakened the chest
the mouth was filled with spittle and foam ...
a brown cloud covered the land like a cloak..
an evil wind that overwhelms the land

it came from the heart of Enlil ... in the west it was spawned ... [the product of] a lightning flash ... an evil blast heralded the baleful storm

Chapter X: FINALE Lying northwest of devastated Shumer, barely touched by the cloud of death, stood proud Babylon, city of MAR.DUK. He convinced the remaining nobles, reeling from the result of opposing him, to proclaim him their supreme lord. He consolidated political power. He revised the assignments of planets, claiming and renaming NI.BI.RU for himself. He had a new creation epic written, with him as its focus.

Marduk predicted that his would be a glorious age, but it actually was a time of turmoil in the region ... in part because of the earthquakes, volcanoes, and famines that struck the Middle East and the Mediterranean basin. The shift of power from AN.UN.NA.KI nobles to human kings, going on for some time, accelerated. Human rulers for the first time waged war, plundering and destroying totally on their own.

The few remaining gods instigated a final series of wars; they seemed not to realize that the reign of their kind was ending. In the regional melee, Babylon was twice sacked and restored and the kingdom of Israel was occupied, its population scattered. Finally, a monotheistic king from the east, Cyrus, was welcomed with his army into Babylon.

So ends The Mesopotamian Tale.

The Mesopotamian Tale

With Commentary

Chapter I: ANOTHER PLANET In the cold of deep space, far, far from the Sun, dwells a now forgotten member of our family of planets. Once every 3,600 years, like a comet, it comes near. This planet was famous in Mesopotamia for the fateful way it crossed the inner Solar System. In fact, one of its many names was The Planet of the Crossing, NI.BI.RU, in Shumerian, the first language of Mesopotamia. The planet was riveting when it approached, for NI.BI.RU appeared as a great golden orb, its brilliance rivaling the Sun.

Astronomers are now searching for a distant planet, a large undiscovered member of our Solar System. They are certain that it's out there and heading in our general direction, because of its gravitational signature on the outermost bodies of the known system. Astronomy buffs call it Planet X. Its highly elliptical orbit may be unique for a planet in our system, but as it happens, not uncommon in the Galaxy. Astronomers studying the systems of nearby stars have found numerous planets whose orbits are elongated ellipses, like the orbits of comets.

Planets coalesce out of loose matter while moving in circles around their suns. The extra-solar planets with elongated elliptical orbits were flung from their original circular paths by gravitational interactions within their systems, as if by slingshot. That's what must have happened to Nibiru.

To the Mesopotamians the planets were powerful bodies of consciousness, celestial deities. With its majestic orbit and its brilliance, NI.BI.RU was deemed to rule the Solar System. As it passed by, if The Planet of the Crossing didn't come close, there could be drama in the heavens, but nothing more. Yet if NI.BI.RU came too near, it would disrupt Earth's atmosphere, crust, and ocean. This was a god to be reckoned with.

From the Mesopotamian texts we deduce that Nibiru's last visit was in 556 BCE. Its next passage, therefore, will be in the year 3,044.

Chapter II: COLLISION The Mesopotamians knew that in the distant past, a water-rich, life-supporting planet had existed, circling the Sun between Mars and Jupiter. Their name for that world was TI.AM.AT, meaning Maiden Who Gives Life. When NI.BI.RU made its transits of the Solar System, it crossed the ecliptic, the plane in which all the other planets spin, in the same way every time: it always transected the path of TI.AM.AT. On one fateful crossing, NI.BI.RU came so close to TI.AM.AT that one of its moons crashed into her, tearing off a portion of her crust. The impact drove TI.AM.AT into an orbit closer to the Sun. Wounded and relocated, TI.AM.AT earned another epithet: KI, meaning Hollowed Out, their name for Earth. In the orbit that had been TI.AM.AT's, the rocky debris from the collision spread out, forming a ring.

We call those rocky bodies asteroids and the ring they form, the Asteroid Belt. The prime candidate for the scar resulting from the collision of Nibiru's moon with our planet is the basin of the Pacific Ocean. Accounting for over a third of the surface of our world, it bears marks of a violent birth: its western chasms, by far the deepest openings in Earth's crust, and the volcanoes and earthquake zones that surround it, the Rim of Fire.

In recent years astronomers have concluded that there have been several major rearrangements in our family of planets. According to the Mesopotamian texts, Earth claimed its present orbit through one such reorganization.

The creation epics of Mesopotamia speak of the collision as a battle between two powerful deities, NI.BI.RU, a hero avenger, and TI.AM.AT, a miscreant troublemaker. In the words of the epic from Babylonia:

[heroic Nibiru] tore Tiamat's [bottom part] to form the great band as a hammered bracelet

Echoes of the Mesopotamian accounts of the collision are heard in the opening passages of the Hebrew Bible. To condense the King James translation slightly:

In the beginning God created the heaven and the earth
And God said let there be a firmament in the midst of the waters ... And God called the firmament heaven

The Hebrew patriarchs came out of Mesopotamia. Their origin is reflected in the scriptures of the faith they founded. The authors of the Book of Genesis folded then-ancient Mesopotamian reports of the momentous event involving two planets into their new tale of cosmic creation.

The word in biblical Hebrew rendered above as *firmament*, *raki'a* (used in modern Hebrew for *sky* or *heaven*) actually meant *beaten surface* ... such as a goldsmith might hammer out. That's a close translation into Hebrew of the term in the Babylonian epic for the Asteroid Belt, *hammered bracelet*. And the biblical term rendered in English as *heaven*, *sham ma'im*, actually means *where waters were*, that is, the place in the sky where the waters of Tiamat once had a home.

To the Hebrew scribes the history recorded by the Mesopotamian scribes thousands of years earlier was not to be totally discarded. The tales from the past must have had the ring of truth and the feel of treasured keepsakes. Yet the Bible's authors used them only in fragmentary, esoteric ways, as in the examples above...introducing into the Bible a layer of meaning hidden from most readers. Perhaps it didn't seem fitting for other than learned members of society to know how the new scriptures of the deity ruling the universe were tied to olden accounts of the deified planet ruling the Solar System.

The Hebrew Bible recorded the theology of an emerging age, a time when, as we shall see, the rule of civilized humanity by the living gods was fading. Written words served as a bridge between the two eras, and by studying the Bible today, we walk that bridge.

Chapter III: CRISIS ON NIBIRU The Planet of the Crossing is home to an advanced humanoid race, tall beings living immensely long lives. The surface of their sunless world was made habitable by a reflective golden shell high in its atmosphere.

Nibiru was still in its original circular orbit (probably the one that now belongs to Earth) when its scientists learned that giant planets of the system were going into a conjunction that would produce a gravitational slingshot, propelling their world far from the Sun. The people had to have gone underground to survive the cataclysm of ejection. Evidently, their engineers were able to deploy a shell of minute particles of gold surrounding the planet. By reflecting artificially generated heat, the shell enabled the population to live on the surface. It also made Nibiru shine brilliantly when it passed near the Earth.

An environmental crisis loomed: the golden shell was failing, but the planet's gold supplies were depleted. An

explorer had earlier found gold on Earth. An expedition was organized. If enough of the mineral could be mined on Earth and sent back home, the crisis could be averted. The king of NI.BI.RU, AN, meaning Heavenly One, chose as leader of the mining colony the eldest of his sons, a prince born to his concubine. A gifted scientist and engineer, he would be called EN.KI, meaning Lord of the Earth. This took place about four hundred fifty thousand years ago ... long before the age of man.

EN.KI, firstborn of divine An, led the colonists as their "great brother"; taught them metallurgy, brick making, building construction, and shipbuilding; made the Tigris and Euphrates navigable and clear; connected the rivers with a canal; and opened waterways in the marshes. (A major Shumerian poem in EN.KI's voice lauds these accomplishments.)

The Anunnaki chose a locale (near present-day Basra) for their settlement because of its many advantages: the nearby marsh was thick with giant reeds, twenty feet tall (growing there still) for crafting the first buildings and boats; the ground held clay with which to make bricks and pottery; near its surface were petroleum substances, a source of energy; to the north, on a broad plain, spacecraft could glide to land; and access to the sea meant that gold could be brought from distant sites.

***Chapter IV: SETTLING ON EARTH** In Shumerian, the settlers were called the AN.UN.NA.KI, Those of Heaven Who Are on Earth. In Akkadian, the next language to develop in the region and the first of the Semitic tongues, they were the I.LU, the Lofty Ones. The colonists named their first settlement E.RI.DU, meaning Home Faraway. The region surrounding E.RI.DU was E.DIN, meaning Home of the Righteous Ones.*

Mesopotamian epithets are still with us. *Eridu* is the source of our planet's name in several languages: *Erde, Arde, Jord, Eretz, Earth. Ilu* evolved into designations for the Divinity in the later Semitic tongues: *Allah* in Arabic and *El* in Hebrew. *Edin* was retained as the name of God's garden in the Book of Genesis. *Ki*, Shumerian for Earth, is the source of the root *geo*.

EN.KI determined that gold mining would be successful. AN sent more colonists, led by a son with his queen, a prince outranking EN.KI in prestige. He would be called EN.LIL, meaning Lord of the Command. Tensions developed. EN.KI, founder of the colony and AN's firstborn, was unwilling to yield leadership to EN.LIL as his father asked. AN, prepared to lead the colony himself and to make one of the brothers viceroy on NI.BI.RU, travelled to Earth to see the fraternal dispute resolved. The three royals drew lots and EN.LIL was the winner. Authority over the colony was to be divided. EN.KI would be chief of all technical matters, lord of the oceans and EN.LIL's subordinate.

Just below EN.LIL and EN.KI in a social system of many ranks were ten AN.UN.NA.KI nobles. Together they constituted a ruling council of twelve, six male, six female. The AN.UN.NA.KI were astrologers, and to them the number twelve governed the Solar System. A circle of twelve governing Lofty Ones would benefit their society by aligning it with the celestial order.

The Lofty Ones counted twelve major bodies in the system: the nine planets, plus the Sun, the Moon, and Nibiru. They saw that the plane of the ecliptic, projected onto the stars, contains twelve constellations, the signs of the Zodiac.

Though EN.KI did at times defy EN.LIL's orders, most disagreements between the brothers were well managed. Dynastic opposition, though, was a fact of life on NI.BI.RU, and it soon characterized the culture of the Earth colony. The descendants of EN.KI claimed that their clan's rights had been usurped when EN.LIL was made supreme ruler. Conflicts over power and prestige arose frequently between descendants of the brothers. Aristocrats came into fierce, jealous opposition, leading to endless battles waged for rights, glory, and riches.

Anunnaki culture was a mold giving shape to the human civilization that would later arise and be characterized by wars begun and led by lust-driven elites.

Chapter V: CRISIS ON EARTH *Ingots of gold were flown to NI.BI.RU every 3,600 years, when the shining planet approached. The mines and smelters in southern and eastern Africa were in full production. The working conditions in the mines, however, were brutal. Suddenly, having borne a hard fate for a very long time, the ordinarily obedient commoners had had enough, and mutinied. A Babylonian epic begins with these words:*

when the gods like men bore the work and suffered the toil the gods' toil was great ... the work was heavy the distress was much ... suffered the toil day and night ... complaining backbiting grumbling

NI.BI.RU was still in need of gold. EN.LIL left E.DIN to see for himself what was happening in the mines and was taken hostage. The epic continues, quoting the leader of the rebellion:

Let us adopt hostilities and battle ... the lofty ones heeded his words they set fire to their tools ... at the gate of the hero enlil ... some shouted let us kill him ... break the yoke

AN came to Earth and convened a council. EN.LIL said he'd resign and return to NI.BI.RU unless the leader of the mutiny was executed, but to AN, the miners' case was compelling. He insisted that a solution be found.

EN.KI envisioned a way to resolve the impasse. He'd observed hominin creatures in the nearby wilds, small and primitive, yet similar to their own race in many ways. He boldly proposed a solution: he would use AN.UN.NA.KI "essence" to modify the native creatures for service in the mines. His partner in the laboratory effort would be NIN.MACH, meaning Great Lady, half-sister to himself and to EN.LIL, a scientist and royal midwife. Gaining EN.LIL's grumpy assent, AN told the pair to proceed.

Many Mesopotamian texts make it clear: the Anunnaki crafted the human race to perform their labor. Between the lines of their poetry we can read what was involved: advanced genetic manipulation of the hominin predecessor of *Homo sapiens*, known to us as *Homo erectus*; in vitro fertilization; and, at first, surrogate birth mothers.

let [Ninmach] fashion a worker
let a workman bear the toil of the lofty ones
let her create a mixed worker let him bear the yoke ...
[all that is needed is to] bind upon [the creature] the image of the gods it can be done ...

*they summoned and asked the goddess the midwife
of the gods ... you are the birth goddess ... make a
primitive worker ... let him bear the yoke assigned
by Enlil*

*let primitives be crafted after [a god's] pattern
out of his blood they fashioned mankind
it was a work beyond comprehension ...*

*in the essence god and man shall be bound to a unity
brought together so that in the end of days the flesh
and the soul which in a god have ripened that soul
in a blood kinship be bound*

After a prolonged time of trial and error, the new race was born. EN.KI's wife was the first surrogate birth mother. Next, fourteen female AN.UN.NA.KI served as surrogates. And so:

*into the wombs of the twice-seven birth goddesses
the mother goddess put the mixed essence ...
the fateful tenth month was approaching ...
she opened the womb her face brightened with joy ...
that which was in the womb came forth*

***NIN.MACH** was revered in Mesopotamia for her role in the birth of humankind. She was also known as **MAM.MU**, meaning Mother Goddess, and as **NIN.TI**, meaning Lady Life.*

There is an obvious linguistic connection between the Mesopotamian mother goddess of humankind, *Lady Life*, and the mother of humankind in the Hebrew Bible. The mate of *Adam*, (Hebrew for *Earthman*) is *Chava*, Hebrew for *Life*. The Jews gave their mother-of-mankind figure the same name that the Shumerians, thousands of years earlier had given to theirs.

And there is a subtle linguistic connection, too: the root *ti*, as in *Ninti*, had a second meaning in Shumerian. (In that language, a word's meaning depended on its context.) *Ti* could also mean *rib*. So *Ninti* could be read as either *Lady Life* or *Lady Rib*. The story of God's creation of Eve from Adam's rib constitutes a link to the Mesopotamian creation epics via a pun (which was a common literary device in Shumer).

In confirmation of the Mesopotamian tales, Zulu oral tradition proclaims that there once were gold mines in Zimbabwe worked by flesh and blood slaves crafted by the first people on Earth.

***Finally, EN.KI** was able to give the servant race fertility, but not the long lifespan of the Lofty Ones. An epic states:*

With his own seed [Enki] made the perfect ... earthling ... with [knowing] he perfected him to him he had given knowing lasting life he did not give

Perfect signified *fertile*. *Knowing* meant sexual activity, as later it would in the Bible. The denial of great longevity to the servant race was an important decision, one that warranted inclusion in Genesis, where it says: ... *behold the man is become as one of us, to* know ... *now lest he put forth his hand and take also of the tree of life and eat and live forever ... [he will be driven from Eden].*

It's no wonder that conventional Science and traditional Faith hold firmly to their positions; they are both correct, up to a point. We were in fact naturally evolved, to the level of *Homo erectus*, and we were in fact *made in the image and likeness of God*, as Genesis terms our resemblance in form and function to the Divine ... because through genetic manipulation we actually were crafted to resemble the Annunaki.

Chapter VI: GIANTS IN THE EARTH The new Earthman was distinct from the two species that had been blended to bring him into existence, the four-to-five-foot-tall, dark, furry, forward-leaning African hominin, and the fair, 7-foot-tall, smooth-skinned, erect being from NI.BI.RU. Intermediate in height between the two, the human beings had features of each ... a head of dark terrestrial hair and a smooth alien skin, for example.

The Mesopotamian Tale reveals that our gnawing questions about our purpose and identity had their source in the manner in which we appeared on Earth. We are the only being ever to exist that had not evolved into an environmental niche. Genetically determined instincts that rule primate behavior had been disrupted, and guidance by a society of our own kind was not to be had, so we entered the world not knowing how to behave in it. We sensed a divide between a lesser being within ourselves and an advanced being. We had feelings of inadequacy from our terrestrial part, and feelings of not belonging from our alien part. The human condition got its start in our shame and uncertainty regarding our nature and our role.

The AN.UN.NA.KI commoners in Mesopotamia asked that humans be brought out of Africa so that they, too, would be relieved of labor. EN.KI objected, so EN.LIL assaulted his compound. His attack succeeded. EN.LIL then took "black headed ones" to E.DIN, where they became laborers, farmers, builders, and cooks.

The first movement of human beings from the birthplace of the race was one of the events that deserved mention in the Hebrew Bible, though the account had to be revised so that it would support the new world view: *and the Lord ... took the Adam and He placed him in the Garden of Eden, to till it and to tend it.*

Cities were founded on the plain and uplands of the rivers Tigris and Euphrates, as settlement moved inland from E.RI.DU, which was near the head of the Persian Gulf, cities such as Ur, Lagash, Nippur, Kish, and Babylon. Enthralled with the tall, brilliant, skilled, beautifully clothed, fair Lofty Ones, the humans living in the cities, materially dependent, inferior physically as well as intellectually, short-lived, dark, and naked, did not need to be coerced into serving their superiors.

To us, the human population of Mesopotamia was bound in slavery; to them, they were occupying their assigned role in the natural order. Inferiority, dependency, and humiliation formed the first sense of self for civilized humanity. That set of beliefs about ourselves was useful for our lords ... and fateful for us. It produced an exaggerated sensitivity to shame, an instinctual response that had evolved to provide functional benefits and also the biological core of a host of negative emotions.

Having become unnaturally prone to feel shame-based emotions, and lacking skills to deal with those feelings rationally, civilized humanity developed many harmful behaviors and attitudes, from addiction to xenophobia, attempting to evade shame emotions. Another layer was thus added to the developing human condition.

The AN.UN.NA.KI, flying from place to place and into the heavens in "sky chambers" and bearing "thunderbolt" weapons, claimed divinity for themselves. In fact, several of the most highly ranked of the Lofty Ones claimed to be the personifications on Earth of the celestial deities, the planets of the Solar System and the signs of the Zodiac.

Thus it came to pass that the rulers of civilized humanity were not just feared, obeyed, and loved...they were worshipped as gods. Civilized humanity started out with superior beings ruling Earth, misrepresenting themselves as deities. That eventually led to a reverse misperception: the personification of the One ruling the Universe. That grave distortion of spiritual reality has plagued the monotheisms from their beginnings. The personification of the Deity came to involve a holdover of the violent nature of the deified Annunaki, making the monotheistic faiths prone to support mass violence ... another aspect of the human condition.

The overall authority for each city rested with one of the twelve highest AN.UN.NA.KI lords. He and EN.LIL together appointed a noble of lesser rank to administer the city as its king. Kingship had been granted to the colony by AN. On Nibiru AN's insignia were the tiara, for his royal stature; the scepter, for his power; and the shepherd's staff, for the guidance he provided. Replicas of the symbols of his authority were given to the kings on Earth.

In the human cultures that were to arise, authority would be divided. The kings of the West would inherit the crown and scepter, and with them a divine right to govern. The bishops would inherit the staff, along with the right to rule over doctrine.

In addition to being the laborers of the cities, humans were the foot soldiers in the armies of the Lofty Ones. For this role, too, no coercion was needed. To fight and die for one's beloved god and to kill the followers of his enemy were glorious deeds.

Battle-trauma, endlessly repeated, spread from the warriors to their kin and to society at large. Civilized humankind began to function much like a person locked in trauma: numb yet over-reactive; self-destructive; prone to violence; relating poorly in physical and social environments; and challenged to learn from experience. Contagion spread trauma between individuals, groups, and generations. In addition, brain circuits never meant to connect, neural pathways governing loving devotion and pathways involved in murderous rage, became interconnected, creating the potential to love war itself. Thus, chronic trauma and an attachment to warfare became additional components of the human condition.

While the noble AN.UN.NA.KI males had female partners, hardly any of the commoners did. The ordinary AN.UN.NA.KI began to take human women as wives ... resulting in an unplanned second round of hybridization between the terrestrial and alien species. Many of the fruits of those unions had greater size, intelligence, and longevity than humans had ever known.

Befitting its weighty impact on humanity, Genesis reported this development free of theological revision: *Those who came down were in the earth in those days ... the sons of the gods came in unto the daughters of men and they bare children to them ... mighty men of old.* The clarity of the passage has been too much for the translators, though. They have consistently rendered *those who came down* as *giants* and *sons of the gods* as *sons of God.*

As a result of the unplanned interbreeding, the human population acquired an unnaturally wide range of endowment. The masses of humanity were no longer inferior only to the Anunnaki, but also to elite humans, taller, smarter, and longer lived than all the rest.

But the *mighty men* had to be insecure in their status, even if subconsciously, for like all humans, they bore the imprint of humanity's original servitude. This led to another aspect of the human condition: the exploitation and subjugation of less endowed people by their superiors…people whose inner slave mentality inclined them to be heartless and blind regarding the plight of the less gifted.

Many humans lived far from the cities of the gods. Since the Anunnaki were unconcerned about humans who weren't under their control, those peoples don't appear in the Mesopotamian texts. Descended from the bands who'd slipped away from Enki's compound in Africa and from groups who later departed from Mesopotamia, they became the indigenous and nomadic tribes of the world. Those peoples are, therefore, the offspring of escapees from civilization…not at all how we think of them.

Chapter VII: DELUGE The AN.UN.NA.KI were thriving, supported in luxury by their enthralled human servants. But disaster loomed. The Lofty Ones learned that on its next passage NI.BI.RU would come close to Earth, wreak havoc, and cause a watery catastrophe. Before the deluge would strike, the Lofty Ones could take to their spacecraft ... yet what of the humans?

EN.LIL had long before then come to regard humankind as an abomination, out of disgust for the interbreeding between humans and AN.UN.NA.KI. He'd even tried to decimate civilized humanity, but EN.KI had blocked his cruel campaigns. Now a natural event was going to do the job for him ... as long as the people were kept in the dark. EN.LIL directed the ruling circle to swear an oath not to disclose the disaster to come, thus sealing the fate of the peoples of Mesopotamia. EN.KI initially refused the oath, but eventually gave in.

However, EN.KI couldn't actually accept the total annihilation of his Mesopotamian children. He designed a vessel that could save a few souls from the city of Shuruppak so that the population of civilized humanity could in time be restored. The craft would also carry "seeds of life", genetic material from the culture's animals and plants. He gave instruction to an esteemed devotee, using a trick to avoid overtly breaking the oath. Keeping the craft's true purpose secret, the follower enlisted help to build it.

This is the sequence of events in the flood epics of Mesopotamia • The golden planet approaches • The Anunnaki learn of the impending flood • A powerful gale blows from the south • A loud roar fills the air • Clouds darken the sky • The Lofty Ones ascend • After massive rains, comes a wall of water.

We can surmise what caused the inundation. Around 11,000 BCE, when these events took place, Earth was in a warming phase that involved, as atmospheric warming is causing now, heavier precipitation, rising seas, and polar ice instability. As Nibiru drew near, interactions - gravitational, magnetic, and electrical - produced storms, earthquakes, and volcanoes on Earth. Temperature-related instability of the Antarctic ice cap plus sudden rains lubricating the ice, plus upheaval of Earth's crust, caused a major portion of the icecap to break off and plunge into the sea. That produced a tsunami dwarfing the ones we've witnessed in our times, moving north through the Atlantic, Pacific, and Indian oceans ... the source of flood legends around the world. As the water surged into the Persian Gulf, it plowed up the sediment that had been deposited by the Tigris and Euphrates at the head of the gulf ... so Mesopotamia was not only drowned, it was buried in mud.

After NI.BI.RU passed over, the AN.UN.NA.KI watched in horror and grief as all they'd built and nurtured in Mesopotamia was obliterated.

the gods cowered like dogs crouched against the outer wall [of the craft a goddess] cried out like a woman in labor ... the anunnaki gods weep with her ...their lips drawn tight ... one and all

Ninti saw and she wept ... my creatures have become like flies they fill the rivers like dragonflies

As the water drained off, they spotted the vessel of salvation. EN.LIL was furious over the violation of the oath. He was urged by EN.KI and the others to relent, and he did ... and pledged to never again harm humankind.

With a rainbow, God made the same promise at the end of the story of the flood in the Book of Genesis. The biblical saga, weaving fact and fiction, gave the Jews an account that helped to preserve the history that had been passed down to them ... while also helping to replace the memory of the Lofty Ones with awareness of the One.

The flood was a dividing line in the history of Mesopotamia; many texts from the time after the deluge specifically refer to persons and developments before the flood. The roots of the culture of the Hebrews were in Mesopotamia; the destruction of the region and its people was too important to ignore, yet too terrifying to think clearly about, hence the need for a revised version.

***Chapter VIII: REBUILDING** If the AN.UN.NA.KI were to once again have the way of life they'd been enjoying, the tasks ahead were staggering. As EN.KI and EN.LIL contemplated rebuilding the cities, restoring agriculture, and resuming gold shipments, they came to a* momentous decision. No longer would humans be restricted to relatively low-level tasks. As the population was rebuilt, promising humans would be endowed with the knowledge and skills needed to restore and maintain civilization. There would be human scribes, scientists, technicians, teachers, artists, musicians … and even kings, for AN decreed that kingship would again be granted to Earth. Each city would have its ruling Lofty One and, as before, he and EN.LIL would jointly summon a king to the throne. Only now the sovereign would be a "man of renown", descended from the marriages of high-ranking AN.UN.NA.KI with humans also distinguished by lineage.

It would take time for the mud left by the flood to dry so that the cities could be rebuilt, food production could rise, and the population could be restored … about four thousand years. A new spaceport, though, was needed quickly, because the two in Mesopotamia were buried deep in soft mud. In the central Sinai a base serving the AN.UN.NA.KI ruling Egypt had survived, but it was too distant from the settlements being restored. A new facility was built in the mountains to the west of Mesopotamia.

That site, *Baalbek*, meaning *Cleft of the Lord*, survives as a ruin. Its launch platform (according to Arab legend, built by a race of giants shortly after the flood) later served as the base for temples built in layers by Shumerians, Akkadians, Assyrians, and Babylonians. When the Greeks and Romans built their own temples on the platform, they made it a place that now epitomizes the culture of the West emerging from the culture of Mesopotamia.

New cities were built on the sites of the buried settlements, their principal edifices built to conform to the *plans and locations of the destroyed originals. Within a few hundred years of their construction, the cities had all the attributes of civilized life: wheeled vehicles and draft animals; boats of various types; canals for irrigation and transport; baked bricks and paved streets; libraries, temples, granaries, schools, and multi-story houses; various metals; fine textiles; domesticated stock, grains, and fruits; musical scales and instruments; judges and juries; civic administrations with bicameral legislatures; money, measures, and weights; commerce, customs duties, and financing; even board games.*

The range of what the cities' scribes wrote is equally impressive: chronologies of dynasties and wars; essays about philosophy, geography, biology, and education; texts of advanced mathematics, astronomy, medicine, surgery, and pharmacology; epics, proverbs, poems, songs, and memoirs; guides for grammar and vocabulary; food and beverage recipes; marriage and inheritance customs; court records and codes of criminal, family, and tax law; commercial records and contracts.

Considering the slow pace of cultural progress in human society (until very recently), such richness should have taken tens of thousands of years to come to fruition. Yet all the above appeared in a few hundred years, the blink of an eye. Scholars note the quandary presented by civilization's flashing fully formed into existence, yet they offer no explanation. They seem confident that science will someday solve the puzzle. That day may be nearing, but only if science accepts what the Mesopotamians said: that civilization was a gift of the gods.

Following the flood, the lands ruled by the AN.UN.NA.KI were divided among the great clans. Mesopotamia proper and its surrounds went to the sons of EN.LIL. Africa was to be ruled by the sons of EN.KI.

The Indus Valley, in present day India, went to IN.AN.NA, granddaughter of EN.LIL. The zone around the Sinai spaceport wasn't assigned to either clan; it went to NIN.MACH. As sister to both royal brothers, it was hoped that she would be able to keep it neutral.

Chapter IX: CONFLICT AND CATASTROPHE The flood interrupted the noble AN.UN.NA.KI's violence. As the human population recovered, though, the ruling Lofty Ones rebuilt their armies and resumed their bloody ways.

Archaeologists, historians, and linguists have meticulously assembled the history of these times. In their thinking, kings and priests promulgated religions of powerful unseen deities in order to better manipulate the populations they ruled. As of yet they have no way to grasp that a race of flesh and blood giants truly were the power in the land.

If one of the Lofty Ones used his personal weapon, he could obliterate the army his forces were facing. These massacres were recalled in the biblical battles in which God miraculously wiped out forces the Jews were fighting.

MAR.DUK, eldest son of EN.KI, made a startling announcement. His astrologic sign was Aries, the Ram, and since Earth was entering the Age of Aries, he proclaimed that it was time for him to ascend and be acknowledged as the chief of all the Lofty Ones.

Meaning to undo what he saw as the original theft of his father's rights by his uncle, MAR.DUK began drives of conquest, rousing fresh hostility between the two clans. EN.LIL was shocked when he realized that MAR.DUK intended to attack the Sinai spaceport ... and that his army appeared unstoppable.

The prospect of his belligerent nephew having control of one of the two launch facilities so alarmed EN.LIL *that he resolved to deny MAR.DUK the base with the only means available to him: destroying it. Dismissing dire warnings from his brother EN.KI, he empowered two of MAR.DUK's rivals to use the colony's hidden weapons of terror, seven powerful bombs. He also authorized the simultaneous destruction of five small cities just north of the Sinai, with the aim of killing MAR.DUK's son. In the battle epic, the attackers are called Annihilator and Scorcher.*

annihilator to the [launch zone] set his course
the awesome seven without parallel trailed behind ...
he raised his hand the [zone] was smashed
the plain by the [zone] he obliterated...
then emulating annihilator ... scorcher the [road
on the gulf of aqaba] followed the cities he
finished to desolation he overturned them

At this major turning point to humanity, the biblical and Mesopotamian accounts overlap, giving complementary views of events. Five settlements in the western diaspora of Mesopotamia, on the plain south of the Dead Sea, *the five cities of the plain*, were allied under Marduk. They faced forces to their east, loyal to Enlil. In the Book of Genesis, the same five cities constitute one side in *the war of the kings of the west against the kings of the east*, a war that involved a northward cavalry thrust by Abraham, ordered by God. If the historical Abraham took part in a war involving Mesopotamian kings, he would have been serving Enlil, chief god of Ur, for Genesis tells that his father was a priest of the god of Ur. We are familiar with two of the five named cities: Sodom and Gomorra. The Bible's vivid account of their destruction closely parallels the language used to describe the attack by Marduk's enemies in the Mesopotamian saga.

In his fear and rage EN.LIL didn't envision the cloud of death the assault would spawn. Killing vapors drifted east with the prevailing winds, devastating (but not destroying) the cities of southern and central Mesopotamia. The near total collapse of Shumer's culture followed, documented in many lamentation texts…

[a god & his wife] hid in their ziggurat …when they
finally left Ur they saw what had befallen the land
the people like potsherds filled the city streets …
in its boulevards … scattered they lay …
on the banks of the Tigris and Euphrates…
sickly plants grow…all living creatures come to an end …
the [cloud] has crushed the land, wiped out everything

on the land fell a calamity one unknown to man
one that had never been seen before
one that could not be withstood …
it stands beside a man yet none can see it …
there was no defending against the … evil
which has assailed the land like a ghost …
through the door like a snake it glides
through the hinge like a wind it blows in …
those who fled to the streets were struck down in the
streets … cough and phlegm weakened the chest
the mouth was filled with spittle and foam …
a brown cloud covered the land like a cloak..

an evil wind that overwhelms the land

it came from the heart of Enlil ... in the west it was spawned ... [the product of] a lightning flash ... an evil blast heralded the baleful storm

Frightened and demoralized, the Anunnaki fled the rebuilt cities of Shumer. After all they had done to establish human civilization, in just a few days they'd wiped out most of it. And that wasn't all. The Lofty Ones who'd come to Earth were aging faster than their peers on Nibiru, and those born here were aging faster still, some even dying. Why stay much longer?

In the northwest rump of Mesopotamia a few gods remained for another millennium, but the absence of others of their kind from the tablets of the period tends to confirm that most of the Lofty Ones were gone. Either the scribes weren't authorized to report their leaving, or they found the abandonment of humanity too painful to document. Civilized humans had never before been without powerful deities living in their midst.

The Greeks of classical times, inheriting their culture from across the Aegean, overlaid older myths with a new pantheon, adapting several of the Mesopotamian deities (Enki, Lord of the Sea, becoming Poseidon) and adding new gods (such as Ares). Their religion continued the original configuration of the human world, except that people could no longer actually see their gods, but would deal with them through omens, ritual, oracles, poetry, and drama, while their philosophers developed the concept of the One, ignoring the gods. At about the same time, the leaders of the Jews made the One the focus of their emerging religion, while actively working to deny the importance of the olden gods.

Chapter X: FINALE *Lying northwest of devastated Shumer, barely touched by the cloud of death, stood proud Babylon, city of MAR.DUK. He convinced the remaining nobles, reeling from the result of opposing him, to proclaim him their supreme lord. He consolidated* *political power. He revised the assignments of planets, claiming and renaming NI.BI.RU for himself. He had a new creation epic written, with him as its focus.*

The Babylonian epic misrepresented many critical events, intentionally fouling the historical record, the original *big lie* by a power-drunk ruler. Unfortunately, it was the first Mesopotamian creation epic unearthed. Filled with theological propaganda, it strengthened the inclination of scholars to regard the older epics they later found as works of imagination, regarding what they said about the gods. The first epics, though, had actually been given by the Anunnaki to the scribes to be recorded on an enduring medium, so that the human beings of the future could have access to their true history.

Marduk predicted that his would be a glorious age, but it actually was a time of turmoil in the region, in part because of the earthquakes, volcanoes, and famines that befell the Middle East and the Mediterranean basin. The shift of power from AN.UN.NA.KI nobles to human kings, going on for some time, accelerated. Human rulers for the first time waged war, plundering and destroying totally on their own.

The elite had learned organized warfare and governance through domination all too well, thus embedding additional pain into the human condition.

The few remaining Lofty Ones instigated a final series of wars; they seemed not to realize that the reign of their kind was ending. In the regional melee, Babylon was twice sacked and restored and the kingdom of Israel was occupied, its population scattered.

Finally, a monotheistic king from the east, Cyrus, was welcomed with his army into Babylon.

When Marduk took the hand of Cyrus in greeting, it signaled the end of the last culture linked in history and religion with then-ancient Shumer. The decline of the olden religion accelerated. By the end of the 6th century BCE, the tablets no longer reported the doings of the Anunnaki. Civilization's first religion and its first political order, intertwined institutions capped by living deities, had been superseded.

So ends The Mesopotamian Tale.

Epilogue

In the tales of the rule of the Lofty Ones we discern the origins of the troubled state of our kind. We can also use the ancient tales to blaze a path leading out of the condition in which we've been trapped. That possibility is explored in *Evolution Diverted*, the weighty book containing *The Mesopotamian Tale* as its narrative core.

Confidence in ourselves as a race of problem-solvers is fading. Despite our best efforts, we've barely been able to slow the turmoil and destruction we're causing. Time is running out. Recent advances in psychology allow us to connect the history revealed by *The Mesopotamian Tale* with the dysfunction humanity exhibits, by explaining how processes that evolved to be protective can go awry and become dysfunctional.

A principle shared by wisdom traditions, philosophers, and clinicians holds that you can't solve your problems if you don't know who you are and that you can't know who you are if you don't know your origins. As it is for a person, so it is for our kind.

Once released from mass amnesia, with memory for our troubled beginnings restored, compassion for our injured selves will lead us in new directions. *Evolution Diverted* suggests ways in which relief from the human condition can begin. For example:

- When we learn that we struggle with an unnaturally high sensitivity to shame because of the conditions of our species' earliest times … and that those conditions also gave us a heightened vulnerability to trauma … we'll have a chance to scale up the restorative interventions that are already bringing healing to individuals personally burdened by the consequences of chronic shame emotions and chronic traumatization.

- When we realize that the monotheisms are caught in distorted ideas about the One, imprints of the Anunnaki lords' lie that they were divine beings, we'll be better able to grasp that our innate awareness of Source can be experienced without the error of personification. We'll then be in a position to keep religion from ever again being misused to suppress love and to instigate divisiveness.

- When we appreciate that automatic deference, rigid social stratification, and the exploitation of the less gifted by the elite were intentionally imposed upon civilized humankind, we'll no longer be resigned to those malignant tendencies.

- When an awakening, already stirring, gains in power, groups pursuing spiritual, humanistic, and environmental initiatives, will synergistically unify their efforts.

This author hopes the reader will feel encouraged to read the book in which all of the above is explored: *Evolution Diverted*.

The Mesopotamian Tale

Mike Brenner

www.ingramcontent.com/pod-product-compliance
Lightning Source LLC
Chambersburg PA
CBHW020301010526
44108CB00037B/512